Rookie
Read-About® Geography

New Jersey

By Susan Evento

Consultant
Donna Loughran
Reading Consultant

Children's Press®
A Division of Scholastic Inc.
New York   Toronto   London   Auckland   Sydney
Mexico City   New Delhi   Hong Kong
Danbury, Connecticut

Designer: Herman Adler Design
Photo Researcher: Caroline Anderson
The photo on the cover shows Barnegat Lighthouse, Long Beach Island, New Jersey.

Library of Congress Cataloging-in-Publication Data

Evento, Susan.
  New Jersey / by Susan Evento ; consultant, Donna Loughran.
     p. cm. — (Rookie read-about geography)
  Includes index.
  ISBN 0-516-22754-8 (lib. bdg.)   0-516-25928-8 (pbk.)
  1. New Jersey—Juvenile literature. 2. New Jersey—Geography—Juvenile
literature. I. Vargus, Nanci Reginelli. II. Title. III. Series.
  F134.3.E95 2004
  974.9'044—dc22
                                        2004000471

CHILDREN'S PRESS, and ROOKIE READ-ABOUT®,
and associated logos are trademarks and or registered trademarks
of Scholastic Library Publishing. SCHOLASTIC and associated logos
are trademarks and or registered trademarks of Scholastic Inc.
1 2 3 4 5 6 7 8 9 10 R 13 12 11 10 09 08 07 06 05 04

Which state is called the Garden State?

Farm stand

New Jersey is the
Garden State!

New Jersey is in the
northeastern part of the
United States.

Can you find New Jersey
on this map?

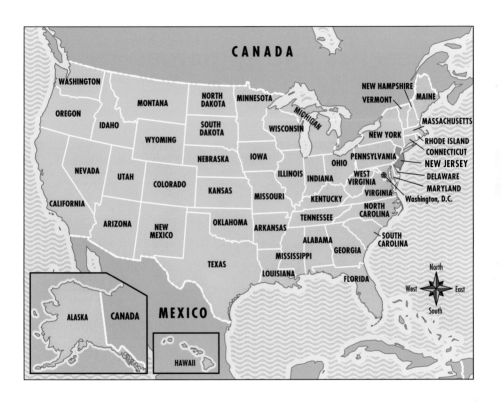

CANADA

WASHINGTON

OREGON

IDAHO

MONTANA

NORTH DAKOTA

SOUTH DAKOTA

WYOMING

NEVADA

UTAH

CALIFORNIA

ARIZONA

COLORADO

NEW MEXICO

MINNESOTA

WISCONSIN

MICHIGAN

IOWA

NEBRASKA

KANSAS

MISSOURI

OKLAHOMA

ARKANSAS

TEXAS

LOUISIANA

MEXICO

ILLINOIS

INDIANA

OHIO

KENTUCKY

TENNESSEE

MISSISSIPPI

ALABAMA

GEORGIA

FLORIDA

NEW HAMPSHIRE

VERMONT

MAINE

MASSACHUSETTS

NEW YORK

RHODE ISLAND

CONNECTICUT

PENNSYLVANIA

NEW JERSEY

WEST VIRGINIA

DELAWARE

VIRGINIA

MARYLAND

Washington, D.C.

NORTH CAROLINA

SOUTH CAROLINA

North

West   East

South

ALASKA   CANADA

HAWAII

5

Farmers in New Jersey
grow fruits and vegetables.
Peaches and tomatoes are
important crops.

Peaches

Flowers in a greenhouse

Farmers also grow flowers such as roses. Many flowers grow in greenhouses that keep them warm in the winter.

New Jersey has different kinds of land.

There are mountains and valleys. There are fields and forests, too.

Kittatinny Mountains

Raccoon

Foxes, raccoons, and black bears live in the forests.

Many birds live there, too.
The American goldfinch
is New Jersey's state bird.

12

The New Jersey coast
is 130 miles long.

People play on the
beach and swim in
the Atlantic Ocean.

New Jersey is the fifth smallest state in the United States.

Most of the people in New Jersey live in large cities.

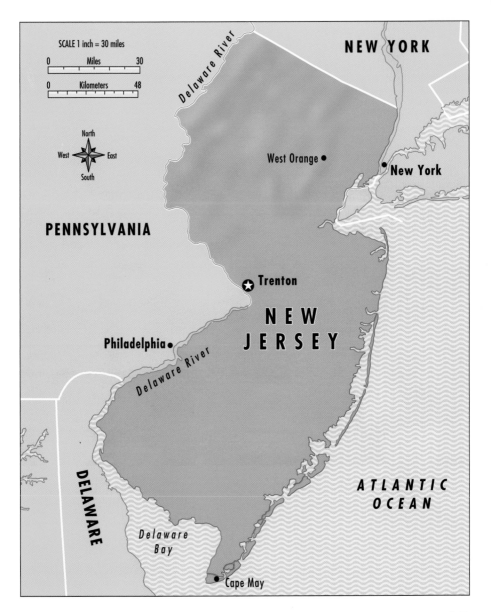

16

Many people who live in New Jersey work in New York City or Philadelphia.

They travel on busy highways to get to work.

There are many factories in New Jersey. Workers make clothing, paper, and medicines.

People also work in hospitals, schools, and other places.

Medicine factory

There are many fun things to do in New Jersey, too.

In the winter, people can ski or snowboard. In the summer, they can hike or swim.

The New Jersey seaside is a great place to visit.

Cape May is a seaside town. Visitors can take boats to look for whales and dolphins.

Whale watching boat

Trenton is the capital of New Jersey.

George Washington worked from here during the American Revolution.

Visit West Orange and you can see where Thomas Edison worked!

Edison was a famous inventor. He invented the light bulb and other useful things.

There is a lot to see and do in New Jersey. Come see for yourself!

Words You Know

beach

goldfinch

greenhouse

highway

raccoon

Thomas Edison

Index

About the Author

Susan Evento is a former teacher. For the past 16 years she has been a writer and editor of books and instructional materials. Recently, she was the Editorial Director of *Creative Classroom* magazine, an award-winning K–8 national teacher's magazine. Evento lives in New York City with her partner and three cats.

Photo Credits

Photographs © 2004: Corbis Images: 7, 30 bottom right (Roger Ball), 27, 31 bottom right (Bettmann), 16, 31 top (Najlah Feanny), 3 (Peter Johnson), 12, 30 top (Kit Kittle), 20 (Bob Krist), 6 (James Leynse), 19 (Robert Maass); Dembinsky Photo Assoc.: 10, 31 bottom left (Skip Moody), 11, 30 bottom left (George E. Stewart); PhotoEdit/David Young-Wolff: 28; Robertstock.com/R. Krubner: 24; Superstock, Inc./Gene Ahrens: cover; The Image Works/Jeff Greenberg: 23; Tom Till Photography, Inc.: 9.
Maps by Bob Italiano.